A Life of Hope

Our Lady
of the
Mississippi Abbey

Founded 1964

Paul Green

A Life of Hope

Our Lady of the Mississippi Abbey

Contents

To have meaning, every human life must have hope. Monastic life is based on a radical hope, a hope for a future in God so glorious that nothing in this world can compare with it. For the sake of this hope, we abandon the possibilities of career and family, and submit ourselves to a highly structured, disciplined life.

Our culture seems increasingly less filled with hope. With the common structures of faith and trust crumbling, more and more people become discouraged and sad. Many fail to find the meaning in their lives that can come only from knowing we can trust in something, in someone, beyond ourselves.

Paradoxically, the limitations and sacrifices of monastic life actually bring us profound blessings. Our guests often speak of the peace they feel as soon as they come onto our property, and ask what makes us so joyful. In these pages we hope to share with you some of our life, some of our joy and hope – and some of the beauty that surrounds us.

We love our world and its beauty, but it is undeniable that our way of life makes no sense if this world is all there is. As St. Paul says, "If for this life only we have hoped in Christ, we are of all people most to be pitied." (1 Cor 15,19).

We are confident that he who calls us is faithful, and he will bring our hopes – and the hopes of all who love him – to a fulfillment beyond our imagining.

David Peterson

Christ among you, your hope of glory.

– Col 1,27

OUR MONASTIC ROOTS

Our Lady of the Mississippi Abbey is part of a long tradition of Christian monasticism, a tradition reaching back 2,000 years to the time of Jesus. Most of our customs and practices were born during centuries of monastic experience in a variety of cultures and climates. Our 21st century monastery belongs to a monastic Order with monasteries on every inhabited continent, sharing a common history.

FOLLOWING JESUS

We trace our beginnings to the early Christian community, the disciples who left behind family and livelihood for the supreme privilege of being in Jesus' presence and soaking up his teaching and his way of loving. After his death and resurrection, while a few disciples became great preachers, the main body of believers just continued to live quiet and simple lives, praying and often eating together, giving whatever possessions they had to be used for the common good, living in joyful expectation of Jesus' return. Very early on some chose to follow Jesus' witness to the future life by giving up marriage and family and devoting themselves to living as Jesus had taught.

In the 4th century AD, after the early centuries of persecution, when Christianity became legal and even socially advantageous, many who wished to live a completely focused Christian life began to withdraw from the larger society. Some organized themselves in communities of women or communities of men; some lived a solitary life, most often in some kind of association with others who chose to live apart. In either case, the desire was to create a culture of evangelical love, an alternative to the unjust society around them. This is considered the true beginning of Christian monasticism as a way of life distinct from that of other Christians. The deserts of northern Egypt in particular hosted vibrant groupings of monastics, whose influence soon spread throughout the Christian world.

ST. BENEDICT

As monasticism spread, it underwent many adaptations to climate and changing social circumstances. In the early 6th century, as much of Europe faced social collapse, an Italian abbot, Benedict of Nursia, wrote a monastic Rule which simplified and codified much of what was best and most humane in the monastic tradition up to that point. Within a few centuries the Rule of St. Benedict had become the norm for monastic life in all of Western Europe, and Benedictine monasteries were havens of peace, learning, and economic stability in a fragmented and often violent world. Above all, the monasteries were the principal source of evangelization and spiritual vitality in the process of transforming Europe from a pagan tribal society to a Christian civilization.

CITEAUX

Our Cistercian family dates from 1098, when 20 monks from the abbey of Molesme, in Burgundy, left their monastery for the usual reason monastics do this kind of thing: they wanted to try a more rigorous and challenging form of monastic life, very faithful to Benedict's Rule. The "New Monastery" they founded, situated in a place named "Citeaux" (Latin "Cistercium," hence, "Cistercian"), also in Burgundy, quickly attracted large numbers of people with a similar desire to live radically for God. Very large numbers: more than 300 new monasteries of monks, and a smaller number for nuns, were founded within the first 50 years.

At the very beginning of this expansion a new organizational system was established to keep the Cistercian reform vibrant and clear [see sidebar]. However, Cistercian women for the most part were not part of the formal organization of the Order. Women in medieval society participated in political and legal systems mainly by virtue of the men to whom they were related (husbands, fathers, brothers). Similarly, our monasteries of women were tied in to the Cistercian Order in an informal way, by a special relationship with a particular monastery of Cistercian men.

But just as women "in the world" also had their own sets of womanly relationships, monasteries of women often had close relationships with one another. Two groupings of Cistercian women's monasteries, one in France and one in Spain, even held their own "general chapters" through much of the 12th and 13th centuries. In fact, some of the oldest continuously Cistercian houses in the world today are monasteries of women. Over time the nuns were formally incorporated into the legal structures of the Order.

The first Cistercians examined every aspect of monastic life in the light of the Rule of St. Benedict, and altered many monastic customs of their time, especially in these areas:

Poverty and manual work. *Being "poor with the poor Christ" included living without luxuries (with a minimum of food and clothing, for example), and restoring manual labor to a central place in monastic life.*

Simplicity. *In addition to a simple lifestyle, this also meant reducing the overgrown liturgical customs of the day. Another quality, still visible in our monasteries today, was a very restrained style of architecture, with minimal decoration, almost no pictures, statues, or use of color.*

Separation from the world. . *Building monasteries well off the beaten track, and severely limiting the access of outsiders to the cloister, fostered the silence and awareness of God's presence necessary for contemplation.*

Unity. *To keep their reform from decaying, Stephen Harding, the third abbot of Cîteaux, under whose leadership the expansion began, devised a system whereby Cistercian monasteries of men would be autonomous, but still strictly responsible to one another through regular visitations and annual meetings ("general chapters") of superiors.*

Heartfelt devotion to Christ. *The second generation of Cistercians, led by Bernard of Clairvaux, pioneered a new spirituality centered on personal intimacy with Jesus. Their writings profoundly touched and influenced the people of their own age and continue to help Christians looking to deepen their relationship with Christ.*

The Chapter Room

THE TRAPPIST REFORM

By 1600, due to a wide variety of circumstances, the Cistercian Order had fallen far from its original spiritual goals. Most attempts at reform were either local or not very long lasting. But in the 17th century a number of French Cistercians, appalled by the decadence they saw in the society around them, began to collaborate in a far-reaching reform that became known as the "Strict Observance." Thanks to the intrepid leadership of its aristocratic abbot, Armand Jean de Rancé, one of our houses of monks, La Trappe, became the standard-bearer of the Strict Observance.

The next challenge our Order faced was the militant atheism of the French Revolution of the 1790's. As the Revolution spread over much of Europe, monasteries were forcibly closed and their members were persecuted. Those who wanted to stay faithful to their religious vows were imprisoned or killed. Some fled, and a number of monks and nuns re-grouped in Switzerland under the leadership of Augustin de Lestrange, a monk of La Trappe. But advancing revolutionary armies soon drove the group, more than 200 strong, across Europe from one refuge to another.

The trauma and violence gripping their world aroused in these monastics a deep sense of the need for penance and conversion. They had seen their whole way of life destroyed, and the group's future remained precarious. At one point in 1799, denied permission to land on either shore, they were living on barges in the Danube. But they stayed faithful to La Trappe's austere program of prayer, silence and fasting as they searched for places to put down permanent roots. God rewarded their dedication by making this group the source of the many "Trappist" monasteries that would spring up in the next two centuries.

THE 20th CENTURY

Many Cistercian houses, especially in central and eastern Europe, were relatively untouched by the Revolution, and had not participated in the 17th century "strict observance" reform. By 1892 the divisions within the Cistercian Order had grown so great that the Trappists split off and formed a separate Order (now officially titled "Order of Cistercians of the Strict Observance" – O.C.S.O.) with its own constitutions, general chapters etc.

Together, our monasteries of monks or of nuns form the only Order in the church with both men and women in the same Order and following exactly the same way of life: a contemplative way, devoted to prayer, community life, silence and manual work. Until recently all of the governing structure of the Order was strictly a male domain, but in the last half-century that has been rapidly changing. Abbesses as well as abbots now participate in the General Chapter which is the "supreme governing authority" in the Order, and together elect the Abbot General (at present, that is still always a monk) who deals with matters between Chapters, and whose permanent council now contains a mix of monks and nuns.

This picture would be incomplete without mentioning that the relationship between our monks and nuns has always been cordial and a tremendous blessing. No human organization is without friction but such frictions as our Order has experienced have not had much to do with the relationship between the genders. All of us are committed to following Jesus Christ in the same monastic way of life.

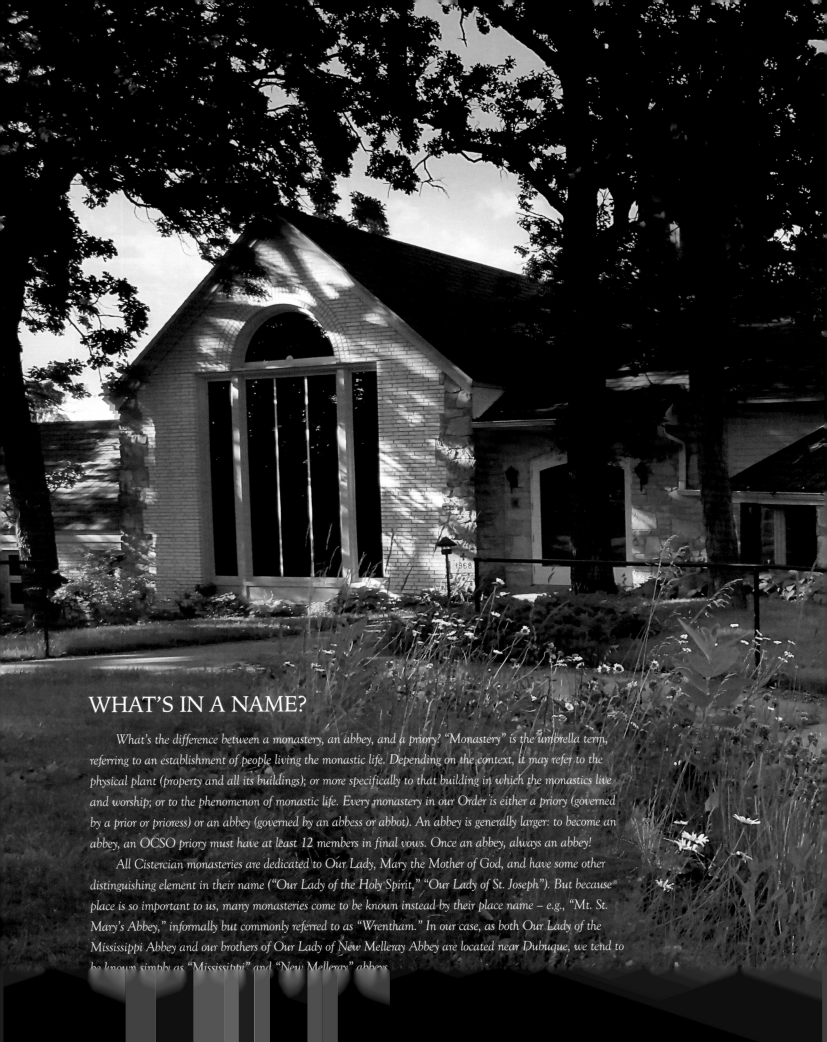

WHAT'S IN A NAME?

What's the difference between a monastery, an abbey, and a priory? "Monastery" is the umbrella term, referring to an establishment of people living the monastic life. Depending on the context, it may refer to the physical plant (property and all its buildings); or more specifically to that building in which the monastics live and worship; or to the phenomenon of monastic life. Every monastery in our Order is either a priory (governed by a prior or prioress) or an abbey (governed by an abbess or abbot). An abbey is generally larger: to become an abbey, an OCSO priory must have at least 12 members in final vows. Once an abbey, always an abbey!

All Cistercian monasteries are dedicated to Our Lady, Mary the Mother of God, and have some other distinguishing element in their name ("Our Lady of the Holy Spirit," "Our Lady of St. Joseph"). But because place is so important to us, many monasteries come to be known instead by their place name – e.g., "Mt. St. Mary's Abbey," informally but commonly referred to as "Wrentham." In our case, as both Our Lady of the Mississippi Abbey and our brothers of Our Lady of New Melleray Abbey are located near Dubuque, we tend to be known simply as "Mississippi" and "New Melleray" abbeys.

1968

OUR FAMILY TREE

In 1802 some of the women in the Trappist group trying to put down roots in the aftermath of the French Revolution established Our Lady of the Holy Cross monastery in Stapehill, England. This is the beginning of our own line. In 1932 Stapehill sent sisters to Glencairn, Ireland to begin St. Mary's Abbey. It grew so quickly that only 17 years later Glencairn made its own foundation, Mount St. Mary's Abbey, in Wrentham, Massachusetts. And with the great influx of post-war vocations, by 1960 Wrentham too was overflowing its buildings. A mere 15 years after its own beginnings Wrentham sent our 13 founding sisters here to Iowa.

We also have two sister houses: our "mother" house, Wrentham, founded Santa Rita priory in Sonoita, Arizona in 1972, and Our Lady of the Angels in Crozet, Virginia in 1987. And we have a cousin in Africa! In 1982 our sisters at Glencairn (our "grandmother") founded St. Justina's Monastery in Abakaliki, Nigeria. Last but by no means least in this saga is our own daughter house, Tautra Mariakloster, which we founded in 1999 on the island of Tautra in Norway, near the ruins of one of our medieval monasteries. Wrentham helped in this endeavor by contributing one of their sisters, a native Norwegian, to the new monastery.

Meanwhile, in 1991, plagued by aging buildings and inflexible building codes, our "great-grandmother" monastery in England transferred to Whitland, Wales, which like Tautra had been home to a medieval Cistercian abbey of monks. England, Wales, Ireland and Norway all had Cistercian women's monasteries in the Middle Ages, but Stapehill/Whitland, Glencairn and Tautra are all the first to be established in their respective countries since the Reformation. Wrentham and Abakaliki have the honor of being the first houses of Cistercian women ever established in their countries.

OUR BROTHERS

Besides our relationship with the women's houses in our lineage, there is another relationship particularly dear to us. Our Lady of New Melleray Abbey, a monastery of Trappist monks in Peosta, Iowa, is only 25 minutes away from us by car – close enough for mutual support, far enough for mutual independence.

Part of the original Cistercian reform was a system of mutual pastoral aid. One of the main sources of this is the system of Fathers Immediate. Every monastery has the abbot of another monastery as "Father Immediate," who

has a certain responsibility of oversight. For monasteries of men, the Father
Immediate is normally the abbot of the house from which they were founded.
New monasteries of women have to find a monastery willing to serve as Father
Immediate; most often, it is the house of monks nearest to them. The Father
Immediate is also responsible for providing the sisters with a chaplain.

Founded from Ireland in 1849, New Melleray is our Father Immediate.
Still more important, from the beginning our relationship has been friendly and
close. In our early years our brothers' assistance was absolutely critical to our
flourishing, and their continued generosity to us has been unfailing. We often
attend one another's solemn professions, funerals, abbatial blessings, etc.; and
we sometimes share teachers, land concerns, and joint projects. We sisters hope
our presence in Iowa and our fidelity to the way of life we all share may in some
small measure repay our brothers for their years of kindness to us.

M. Columba with the foundation cross, and the twelve foundresses, to her left. Sr. Cecile (prioress) and M. Angela (abbess) of Wrentham, and Dom Thomas Keating, abbot of Spencer, accompanied the foundresses to Iowa (on the right).

OUR LADY OF THE MISSISSIPPI ABBEY
– Our Story

FOUNDATION

Mississippi Abbey was founded in 1964, but Mother Angela Norton, abbess of Mt. St. Mary's Abbey in Massachusetts, had begun to hunt for a suitable site several years earlier. Wrentham, constructed to house 60 sisters, was struggling to accommodate more than 70, with new candidates still arriving.

In 1961, after an abortive investigation of some possibilities in Argentina, Mother Angela wrote to the Trappist abbots in the U.S. asking for assistance. Dom Philip O'Connor, abbot of New Melleray Abbey in Iowa, responded with offers of several possible properties. After several years of investigating sites in Iowa and elsewhere, land was purchased about 20 miles from New Melleray. But the new property had no buildings, water, or electricity, and the cost of the project was steadily mounting.

Then one day Dom Jim Kerndt, who succeeded Dom Philip as abbot of New Melleray, read in the *Wall Street Journal* that Hickory Hill Farms south of Dubuque was for sale. A well-kept "farm with charm," it had rolling hills, spectacular views across the river, and best of all, the Stampfer family residence whose large rooms could be converted into a temporary monastery. Mother Angela and Mother Columba, superior-to-be of the new foundation, flew immediately to Iowa and within days New Melleray had purchased the property for us.

There is a monastic saying, "we form our buildings and then our buildings form us." Our monastery proper has grown from the original core of the Stampfer home, with the beautiful views of a hilltop location but all the disadvantages of trying to construct the regular monastic spaces on steeply sloping land. It would be many years before we could afford to build anything like a real monastery, and to this day we lack the cloister and central organization of spaces which are characteristic of most monasteries. On the other hand, there is a hominess, a non-institutional charm, that has become one of our characteristics.

M. Columba Guare, *superior of Mississippi 1964-1982. As our founding superior, she set the course for our community and guided us through the changes following Vatican II. Of all the people who have touched our communal life, her influence has been the greatest.*

M. Angela Norton, *abbess of Wrentham 1952-1986. A former Dominican sister, she transferred to one of our monasteries in Canada. When Glencairn founded Mt. St. Mary's Abbey, she and several other Americans were sent from Canada to join the foundation. Three years later she was elected abbess.*

Dom Matthias ("Jim") Kerndt. *As procurator and then abbot of New Melleray he spearheaded the search for our site. Fr. Jim later served as our resident chaplain for over 20 years, 1980 – 2000.*

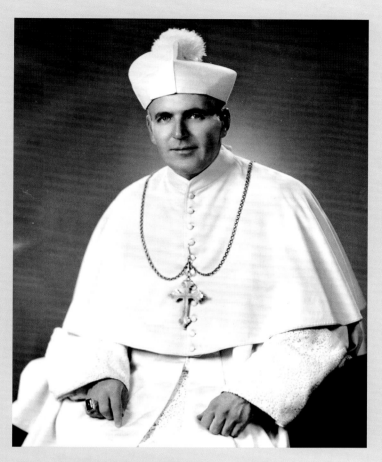

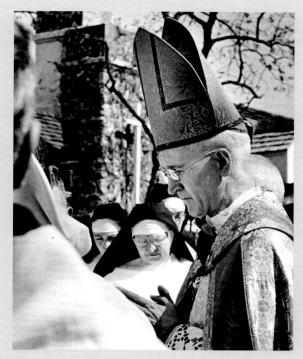

Most Reverend James Byrne, *Archbishop of Dubuque. He gave us the official permission to come to his archdiocese. Until his retirement in 1983 he celebrated Mass for us on Christmas and Easter every year.*

Dom Philip O'Connor. *The abbot who invited us to Dubuque, he remained a good friend of our community. Eight months after we were founded he became our resident chaplain, a post he held for nine years.*

Dr. Joseph O'Donnell. *He donated property near Clinton, Iowa as a possible site for the new monastery; when it proved unsuitable, he gave the proceeds of the sale of the property toward the purchase of Hickory Hill Farms.*

Setting out for Iowa – on a jet plane

Exploring our new property

The monks quickly set about preparing the home to serve as a monastery while M. Angela prepared the personnel and all the other details that go into starting a new monastic community. There is an ancient tradition of sending a superior and twelve others as the starting group, modeled on Jesus and his twelve apostles. Mother Columba Guare was named superior and twelve other sisters were chosen to go on the foundation. The Wrentham community chose the name "Our Lady of the Mississippi Abbey" for their daughter house because it overlooks America's great river.

On October 18, 1964 the sisters arrived in Dubuque. The property was not quite ready, but the business jet of a friend of Wrentham became available that day, so with little warning and less packing the group was off. Dubuque is home to the motherhouses of several congregations of religious women, and they came to our immediate assistance, the start of long relationships of friendship, encouragement and help. After a few weeks of makeshift quarters (and clothing), the first Mass in the new "chapel" was celebrated on November 4, M. Columba's birthday, which we count as our official founding day.

EARLY YEARS

Gradually the main requirements of a monastery were set in place. Our candy business started up in 1965 and fairly soon began to support us. Various New Melleray brothers oversaw our land until in 1967 Br. Placid Zilka was sent to live on our property and manage it full-time. The following year our abbey church was completed and dedicated. With a beautiful space in which to worship God, we were well on our way.

In addition to our unusual building circumstances, two other factors had a formative influence on our monastery. First of all, the founding group was very young and not very seasoned in monastic life: most were in their 20's, and only one sister was older than 40. So there was a great deal of energy on hand, and for decades there was a sense of constant doing and busyness which we struggled to balance with monastic calm and tranquility. In addition, the kinds of work we set in place, and the buildings we built, were not designed for a normal age distribution, but for the abnormal one of our early decades. Only recently, as we finally have a population of elders as well as younger members, are we redesigning our buildings and our work for a broad range of ages.

Second, we were founded just at the end of the Second Vatican Council, as radical changes were beginning to affect religious life. For the Trappists, the big changes came at the very end of the 1960's, and we had to start implementing them when the sisters as individuals and the community as an entity were still young and inexperienced. On the whole we navigated these waters surprisingly well, without, for example, serious loss of membership. The nuns of our Order in general implemented the post-conciliar changes more slowly than the monks, each house of nuns preferring to move ahead as a community with everyone on board, while the monks were more often divided between those who wanted much more change and those who wanted much less. In any case, our identity was formed during a time of great change, and the sense that changes are possible and even normal became part of our makeup.

Most of the post-conciliar changes our monastery would implement occurred between 1968 and 1980. By 1970 we had dropped the gimp and old veil in place of a simpler collar and veil that allowed hair to show, and several sisters had returned to their baptismal names. The grills and walls separating sisters from guests in the church, visiting parlors and entrance slowly disappeared, and we began addressing one another by first name, without the prefix "Sister." For some, one of the most painful changes was

Cornerstone of our church

Novice wearing the old veil and gimp; abbess with new veil and collar

M. Columba and our prioress (2nd superior), Sr. Rosemary

the move from Latin to English in the liturgy, which was done suddenly and without much community input (these were largely pre-dialogue days). On the other hand, the last series of significant changes happened with quite a lot of dialogue. In 1980, with the facilitation of Dom David Bock, abbot of New Melleray, the community decided to begin to permit speech between sisters, and to have a common supply of frequently used items which sisters could now take without writing for permission.

AUTONOMY

Sr. Kathy Lyzotte, the first novice to become a permanent community member

In 1970 our monastery became an autonomous abbey, no longer a dependent foundation of Wrentham: our foundresses formally transferred their stability from Wrentham to Mississippi, and Mother Columba was elected our first abbess. Our novitiate had opened in 1968, but our only novice left in 1970. As three foundresses had also left by that time, the community was then down to 10 members, the lowest figure in our history. But in that very year our Lord in his providence sent us two new women who would become permanent members.

A gradual influx of new members during the 1970's meant we were running out of space. In 1976 our brothers of New Melleray completed a major renovation project, and when we went over to celebrate their beautiful new church, they presented us with a very large check toward our own building project. Mother Columba began raising funds, and in 1977 we broke ground for a major addition which would more than double the size

Sisters carrying produce from the garden below to the monastery on top of the hill

of our monastery and provide us with structures more conducive to monastic life and silence. Building proceeded slowly, and in 1979 we had to stop altogether when funds ran out. Then in October a friend of Dom Philip, Fr. Leo Henkel, gave us a major grant, and on Thanksgiving Day we moved into our new dormitory with individual cells (bedrooms) for each sister. By the spring of 1980 all the construction was done and we had a new refectory (monastic dining room) and library as well.

In 1974 M. Columba became the spiritual director of BJ Weber, a young Dubuque man newly converted to Christ, who lived on our property while studying for ordination as an Evangelical minister. Now an Anglican priest in New York City, BJ and his wife Sheila continue to have a very special relationship with our community. In his ministries to street people, to UN ambassadors, to the Yankees, to couples in need of marriage counseling, BJ considers us his major spiritual support system. It is a two-way relationship: he visits us frequently, introducing us to new friends and advisors, and sharing with us his own exuberant love of Jesus.

For our first 15 years, several large bedrooms in the Stampfer home served as our dormitory. The room shown here housed five sisters, with curtains separating each sister's space. By 1979, there were no spaces left.

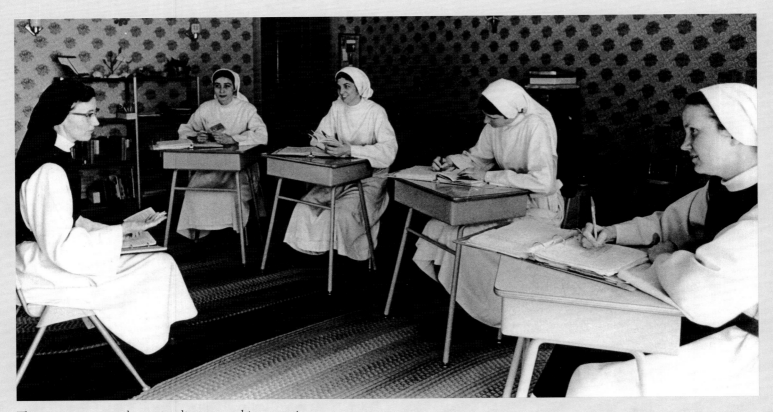

The novitiate room: the novice director teaching new sisters.

New dormitory, under construction, in background.

Early 1980's
Left background: the back of the original Stampfer house
Right background: the church, added 1967-68
Center foreground: the three wings of dormitory and refectory,
    added 1978-79

TRANSITION

The mid 1980's was a time of major transition for us. Having a very different living space and new rules about speech and silence were a part of this transition. But more significant still was our first change of superior. Mother Columba, our leader throughout our first 18 years, resigned in 1982 at the end of her second term as abbess, and M. Gail Fitzpatrick was elected in her place. By mid-1983 we had shrunk from 18 sisters to 13, the biggest loss of membership in our history. However, by the grace of God, and with the steadfast leadership of our new abbess, we quickly recovered and were on the road to future growth. In fact, 1984 - 90 brought us more new members than any other comparable period.

Another major change was the loss of Br. Placid, who returned to New Melleray late in 1985 after 19 years with us. While he ran our farm, we had no need for hired help; moreover, the farm was a major part of the sisters' work as well. A number of us could drive tractors and helped with much of the cultivation, while nearly all of us helped regularly to bring in hay and straw, to "walk" (weed) soybeans, to assist with the oat harvest. Without Br. Placid, we had to cut back drastically on our farming activities and hire part-time farm workers; and the farm was no longer part of our common work.

M. Gail Fitzpatrick is blessed as abbess

The abbess is elected from among the sisters. She receives her power from God through the ministry of the Church.

Constitutions of the O.C.S.O., 33.1

Around this same time our community formed two important friendships. In 1984 Fr. Brendan Freeman was elected abbot of New Melleray. Ultimately he would be our Father Immediate for nearly 30 years – more than half our history. One of the characteristics of our community we haven't mentioned so far is a love of parties – and Fr. Brendan was a natural fit in this respect! As well as being a great source of counsel and a tremendous support to us at all times.

The second friendship was with Br. Ronnie Fogarty, a Marist brother from Australia, who first visited us in 1983 to help our dialogue process. Br. Ronnie was already in his mid-70's, but full of vigor and wisdom. We invited him back repeatedly over the next 16 years, and he revolutionized our process of dialogue and decision-making, helping us to base them on faith in God and awareness of the divine presence. To this day we often refer back to what we learned from this dear friend.

Until 1987 our only bell was an old train bell. Bells are quite expensive, and Archbishop Kucera made an appeal for us in the diocesan newspaper. Our local pastor, Fr. Jim Secora, located an unused bell at Loras College, Dubuque, and arranged for it to be donated to us. Cast in 1927 in Baltimore, our bell was named "Ave Maria," a name all the more welcome to us as 1987 had been proclaimed a "Marian Year." We had a new bell tower constructed and in November Fr. Secora blessed the bell and the tower. To our delight, the sound of our old train bell harmonized with the new bell, so we ring both on major feasts. ~ Ave Maria has separate actions for tolling and pealing. For tolling, the bell remains stationary while a clapper strikes it on the outside. For pealing, the bell is set swinging and hits an interior clapper repeatedly.

MATURITY

By the late 1980's our community had reached maturity, although our median age was still quite young (46.5 in 1990). M. Gail's broad horizons soon brought us into greater contact with our Order at large. She was chosen to be part of a small team working at our General Chapters on the revision of our Constitutions, finally completed in 1990. In 1992 the group of abbots and abbesses which prepares the General Chapter met for the first time in the United States. M. Gail persuaded the participants to visit Mississippi en route to or from their meeting so that we had the privilege of encountering well-known people in our Order from other continents.

We also became involved with a number of other communities. In 1987 M. Gail was part of an Apostolic Visitation requested by our great-grandmother house, Holy Cross Abbey in Stapehill, England. Our former abbess, M. Columba, soon went there as a temporary superior, and over the next 4-5 years a number of Stapehill sisters made prolonged stays or short visits with us, an utterly delightful experience.

In 1989, led by our friend Br. Ronnie, we discerned the possibility of making a foundation and concluded this was not yet God's will for us. Instead we used our abundance of personnel during the next decade to allow one or two sisters at a time to be away for an extended period in the service of our Order. One sister assisted at monasteries in Canada and Belgium; one explored possibilities for monastic life in Norway; one studied theology in Washington; one worked at the Order's central office in Rome; and one acted as temporary superior of our monastery in

Fr. Brendan joins us for a sister's jubliee celebration.

With joy you will draw
water at the fountain
of salvation.

– Is 12,3

Redwoods, California. Meanwhile a series of recently "retired" superiors
from other countries came to us for some months of "rest" after leaving
office, bringing us into closer contact with their monasteries in Belgium,
France, and India.

The 90's also brought physical changes to our monastery, many of
them aimed at improving our reception of guests. We thoroughly
renovated our church in 1991 with new flooring, choir stalls, lectern, altar
and tabernacle, and a new and far better organ. Our cemetery, like much
of the rest of the land on top of our hill, is almost solid rock, and we had
excavated 12 potential graves in 1974. Now, in 1992, we made room for 50
more graves, and two years later beautified the cemetery entrance with an
arch and cross. The only external door in our church was in our guest
chapel, so any time we processed outside we had to wend our way through
its small aisles and door. In 1995-96 we renovated the guest chapel so
there was actually room to process, widened the outside door, added a
bathroom for guests, and put an icon display at the guest entrance. At the
same time we redesigned the paths in front of church so the guests would
no longer pass right in front of our big sanctuary window (which always
made us feel like we were in a fishbowl). The new paths, unlike their
flagstone predecessor, are flat and thus easier to keep ice-free in the long
Iowa winters – a priority especially after one of the local priests broke a leg
on our old walk. The finishing touch was a lovely new landscape in front
of the church, with a fountain at the center. And finally, in 1998, we built
a guest parking lot, using some of the land in front of our candy building.

Sr. Gail, Sr. Ina, Bishop Georg Müller of Trondheim, and Sr. Rosemary at the ruins of the original Tautra Mariakloster, examining a model of the medieval monastery. Sr. Ina, a native Norwegian sister from our monastery of Laval, France, originated the project of re-establishing Cistercian life in Norway.

February 14, 1999. At Vespers, Archbishop Hanus, together with M.Gail and Fr. Brendan of New Melleray, bless the sisters about to set off for Norway. M. Rosemary, superior of the new foundation, holds the foundation cross.

FOUNDING A DAUGHTER HOUSE

Nevertheless, the question of a foundation would not go away, and in 1997 we began a new discernment process. Part of the dilemma for us was the realization that our own monastery still needed some major building work: we finally had sisters using canes or walkers, and there was almost no provision for limited mobility. Our monastery is really 3 separate buildings on different levels: the original house; then, four feet lower, the church; and three feet below the church, the dormitory; while the refectory was on another floor altogether. To go from the church to the chapter room, as we do every day, meant going up a short narrow flight of stairs, or else going outside – if the walks were free of snow.

We didn't have enough funds for even one of these projects. Nevertheless the experiences of our Sr. Marjoe, who had explored the situation in Norway, together with a number of other signs, convinced us that God's will for us now was to make a foundation. After a formal vote approving the project we began to look at possible locations, in Tunisia as well as Norway. In January of 1998 Sr. Gail asked each sister to pray about two questions: where do I think God is calling our community to make a foundation, and where do I think God is calling me personally (Norway, Tunisia, or to stay in Iowa). The answer to the first question was overwhelmingly, though not unanimously, in favor of Norway. With this information, we set aside January 26, the feast of the founders of Citeaux, as a day of prayer for the guidance of the Spirit of Jesus. Two days later, our final vote was unanimous for Norway.

The new foundresses (including 2 of our own original foundresses) were soon chosen, and the next year was spent in preparing for the foundation. With the help of the Catholic bishop of Trondheim and the support of the local people, we were able to purchase property on the little island of Tautra, the site of a Cistercian monastery in the Middle Ages, with some ruins still standing. And in February 1999, five of our sisters, together with two Norwegian sisters from other monasteries, refounded Tautra Mariakloster.

Eye has not seen, nor ear heard, nor the human heart conceived,
what God has prepared for those who love him.   – *1 Cor 2,9*

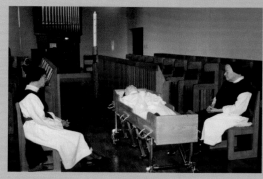

The Paschal candle, sign of our faith in the resurrection, burns as we keep watch with our sister's body.

On Sunday October 29, 2000, our oldest foundress, Sr. Augustine, had a serious stroke, and it was immediately evident that she would not survive. We were able to keep her at home, under the loving care of her own sisters, as she and we waited together for Jesus to come for her. Each of us spent a few moments alone with her saying goodbye, and on Monday evening a tolling bell let us know her last minutes on earth had come. The entire community squeezed into Sr. Augustine's little room and began to pray Compline, the last Office of the day. When we reached the canticle, 'Now, Lord, you dismiss your servant in peace...,' she breathed her last.

In the 36 years of our community life we had never had a death. Sr. Augustine's was a beautiful beginning for us - she even managed to inaugurate our cemetery on All Souls' Day, Nov. 2. We dug the grave ourselves (on Halloween!) with the help of an experienced neighbor. The next day, All Saints, our sister's body was brought into the church, and we took turns watching in pairs with her and praying the psalter all day and night until her funeral. A good crowd of our brothers from New Melleray and of friends joined us for the Mass and procession to the grave site. It is the Cistercian custom not to use a casket but only an open bier. We covered Sister with a cloth before our brothers lowered her into the grave, as we sang the verse each of us sings at our final profession:

"Receive me, O Lord, as you have promised, that I may live;

Do not disappoint me in my hope."

According to custom, the abbess threw in the first shovelful of dirt, followed by several sisters and guests - but we added a little touch of our own, throwing in flowers as well. After a reception for our guests we changed into work clothes to finish filling the grave. As in life, in her death Sister was a model of Christian hope, and each of us looks forward to the day when we too will take our place in the community cemetery. The life of the monastery continues around us, "as we await adoption as God's children, the redemption of our bodies." (Rm. 8,23)

Digging Sr. Augustine's grave.

Procession to the cemetery at the end of the funeral Mass.

Filling in Sr. Augustine's grave.

Tautra Mariakloster, overlooking the Trondheim fjord. The church is on the right..

The next years were some of our busiest. After our own experience as a foundation, we were determined that our daughter house would have a properly built monastery, and so we ran the only major capital campaign we have ever conducted. The community hosted numerous fund-raising events, and some sisters were removed from the regular work force to raise money. Archbishop Jerome Hanus of Dubuque gave us permission to ask the parishes for help, and nearly all of us spent occasional weekends speaking at parishes – not something that comes naturally to contemplative nuns! As none of us is from Dubuque and few from Iowa, this had the benefit of acquainting us for the first time with the local church and making the diocese aware of our presence and our prayers.

At the same time we were still responsible for the little group in Norway, sending one sister or another to help for a few months, and eventually, a sixth sister as a permanent member. Also, we still needed to consider our own building needs, and the early 2000's were filled with visits from architects and attempts at a master plan – none of which seemed workable to us. Since we had neither funds nor energy to take care of all our needs right away, we also had to narrow our focus to the immediate future. The first clear direction came from a friend who took one look at our candy factory and advised us that a good facility for earning our livelihood should be our first priority. After months of intensive planning, we broke ground for our new "candy house" in October 2001 and occupied it in August 2002. The next year we reorganized the interior space of the old candy house, dedicating part of it to hospitality and renaming it "St. Benedict's Welcome Center." How providential that our guest parking lot was already in front of this building!

On the feast of the Guardian Angels, Oct.2, 2001, we broke ground for our new "candy house" and the site was blessed by Archbishop Hanus. Exactly one year later, the completed facility was blessed.

Ground-breaking ceremony

2001

Blessing the new candy house

2002

39

JUBILEE

By 2006 the new monastery in Norway had also been built and Tautra was autonomous; our capital campaign had wound down; and we were relieved to return to our normal obscure and contemplative existence.   With these projects completed, Sr. Gail decided that after four 6-year terms as our abbess, it was time for new leadership in our community, and in May 2006 we elected M. Nettie Gamble as our third abbess.

For our first 42 years we had had only 2 superiors, both of them among our foundresses; now we had a leader who had begun Cistercian life in our midst at Mississippi. During her term in office, we finally renovated our monastery to provide for our seniors. Dave Richen, an Oregon architect who had worked with several of our monasteries on the West coast, came up with a master plan that finally made sense. The steep slopes of our land meant we have tended to build in a long crooked line along the top. But there is a limit to how far we would want to push the ends of the monastery away from each other, and we had already reached it. Early one morning, at the very hour we sisters were starting our daily prayers, Dave woke up with an inspiration for the solution: to build a senior wing alongside the church, nestled in a bend between buildings.

Our library/scriptorium 1980-2009. Since there were no interior supports underneath (the refectory occupied the space below), only the outer walls could support the weight of books. As books accumulated over the years, our book collection was increasingly dispersed to odd rooms elsewhere in the house.

At the same time that we built this senior wing, we also put ramps between all the sections of the monastery. Moreover, since the new wing has a basement we could use for a library, our old library, situated on the same level as the church and senior wing, could become our refectory. All of this meant that for about 6 months in 2009 the community had to vacate the whole monastery except the offices housed in the original Stampfer home. Sisters had beds in various offices or outbuildings, meals were cooked and eaten in the candy house, and the liturgy was celebrated either at St. Ben's or at candy. Our two senior sisters went to live in town with the senior sisters of the local BVM congregation, until one of them, our dear Mother Columba, came home in the midst of the construction to pass her last weeks with us before her death on Sept. 1.

In the midst of all this chaos, Sr. Nettie maintained a peaceful and calm presence which helped us immeasurably, especially after so many years of intense activity. We settled quickly into our new spaces once they were complete. One sister commenting on our new corridors and greater sense of spaciousness said it for all of us: "Now I really feel like it's a monastery!"

The activities of the monastic refectory replicate some of those of the church: the community is gathered, eats, listens to common reading, prays. Traditionally, the refectory also reflects the architecture of the church, so our old library, with its high pitched roof and large wooden cross-beams, makes the perfect refectory.

When a new abbess is installed, each professed sister kneels before her and promises her obedience.

In 2012 we elected our fourth abbess, M. Rebecca Stramoski. With the most pressing needs of our seniors addressed by the new wing and ramps, we have engaged in a serious study of our candy business, as the number of sisters who can do the heavier jobs in the factory has shrunk. The challenge is to continue to support ourselves by the work of our hands without compromising the monastic peace and silence that lead us to God.

The decades since the founding of Tautra have had both blessings and challenges. Giving six capable members, nearly a quarter of our community at the time, to the church in Norway was a sacrifice we made gladly. The many ways God has blessed the new monastery have confirmed us in our belief that this was indeed his will for us. Still, it was unquestionably a sacrifice, and one that was followed by further losses, not least the departure of several members in final vows. And after over 35 years with exceptionally good health and not a single death, we have now said our earthly good-byes to our three oldest members, and a few sisters have been diagnosed with chronic physical disorders. But with all this, we retain wonderful blessings, not least great unity among ourselves, great joy in our calling, and the gift of new members joining us.

Our 50th anniversary of foundation was November 4, 2014, and we decided to begin our jubilee year on the feast of St. Benedict, July 11, 2014. This turned out to be providential in an unexpected way. Sr. Regina, one of our foundresses, had been in our senior wing since it was built. After several years of deteriorating health, very patiently borne, she was hospitalized with an infection which proved intractable. Not long before the opening jubilee celebration we brought her back to the monastery, and she went home to Jesus very peacefully, just after all our jubilee guests had departed. Like our other "graduates," Srs. Augustine and Columba, we trust she is with the Lord, interceding for us – and for all to whom God is opening their hearts in eternity.

Mass for the opening of our Jubilee Year, July 11, 2014

THE MONASTIC WAY

The thirst to give oneself completely to God is at the heart of monastic life. Everything in the monastery is directed to putting Jesus Christ at the center and helping us toward our heart's desire of union with God in love. The Rule of St. Benedict, written around 500 A.D., has proven to be a marvelous spiritual and practical guide for this kind of life. To this day it remains the "Rule" by which Cistercian monastics seek to live out the Gospel.

Behold, in his loving kindness, the Lord shows us the way of life.

Rule, Prologue

THE BENEDICTINE TRIPOD

The Rule rests on a tripod of three activities which fill the monastic's day: prayer, reading, and work. The monastic schedule is structured to move back and forth between these activities, especially between work and prayer.

Prayer

St Paul's injunction, "Pray without ceasing" (1 Thess 5,17) resonates in the souls of all Christian monastics. Our day revolves around times of community prayer, with times for silent personal prayer as well.

Devote yourself frequently to prayer.
Rule, Ch.4

Holy Reading

Christian prayer is unthinkable without time spent pondering the Word of God. Holy reading, or *lectio divina*, is a slow, contemplative way of reading that leads to prayer and begins to align our thoughts with the teachings of Jesus.

They should have specified periods for...lectio divina.
Rule, Ch.48

Work

We work to earn our living, to share the common lot of humankind, and because labor is one of God's gifts. The Cistercian reform emphasized the place of manual work as a way to be poor with the poor Christ; the Trappist reform within the Cistercian Order saw work as one of the disciplines of love.

When they live by the labor of their hands, then they are really monks.
Rule, Ch.48

Only if the sisters prefer nothing whatever to Christ will they be happy to persevere in a life that is ordinary, obscure and laborious.

– Constitutions of the O.C.S.O., 3.5

THE BENEDICTINE VOWS

Benedictine monastics make three vows: stability, obedience, and conversion of life. On the deepest level there is only one vow, the vow to give oneself to God completely, in the monastic way of life and together with one's community. Obedience, stability and conversion of life are critical aspects of that underlying vow.

Stability

We vow to remain all our life with our local community. We give up the temptation to move from place to place in search of an ideal situation. Ultimately there is no escape from oneself, and the idea that things would be better someplace else is usually an illusion. And when interpersonal conflicts arise, we have a great incentive to work things out and restore peace. This means learning the practices of love: acknowledging one's own offensive behavior, giving up one's preferences, forgiving.

> *Stay in your cell, and your cell will teach you everything.*
> Sayings of the Desert Fathers.

Obedience

We vow to obey God, the Rule, our abbess, our community. All of us struggle with blindness and emotional attachments to our own wants and ways of doing things. The goal of obedience is not only a harmonious community, but primarily to assist each sister to grow in freedom from her own ego drives, so she may be united more closely to the will of God.

> *No one is to do what she judges better for herself,*
> *but rather what is better for the other.*
> Rule, Ch. 72

The monk who is to be received into
the community makes these promises
in the presence of all, in the oratory:
stability, conversion of life, and obedience.

– *Rule, Ch. 58*

Conversion of Life

We vow to live a simple, celibate life according to the customs of our
monastery and to be always open to change and to grow. We are to accept with
contentment the basic monastic regimen of our community and live out
community decisions in a cooperative spirit. Above all, we must always be
willing to ask forgiveness, to change our way of thinking and behaving, and to
learn new and more loving ways of relating to others.

Progressing in this way of life ['conversion'] and in faith,
we will run in the way of God's commandments,
our hearts expanding with the unspeakable sweetness of love.

Rule, Prologue

THE BENEDICTINE VIRTUES

St Benedict devotes one chapter to each of three virtues (chapters 5 - 7), the spiritual center of his doctrine.

Obedience

The virtue of obedience helps us transcend our selfishness and self-will. It is not an attitude of "go-along, get-along" but a complete surrender of oneself, above all to God, but on a daily basis to whatever God puts in our life. It is also a kind of radical non-violence, refraining as much as possible from setting one's will and preferences in opposition to those of others, which is the root of all violence.

The labor of obedience will bring you back to him from whom
you had drifted through the sloth of disobedience.

Rule, Prologue

Silence

"Trappist'" means "silent" to many people, and although we no longer observe the almost total absence of speech practiced in recent centuries, we still maintain an atmosphere of silence in which we can be attentive to God at every moment, and grow in self-knowledge. At certain times of the day (evening and early morning) we refrain from all communication with each other, verbal or non-verbal, to help one another toward our goal of continual prayer.

So important is silence that permission to speak
should seldom be granted even to mature disciples.

Rule, Ch. 6

Humility

Humility, the most essential monastic virtue, is a willingness to learn the truth about oneself, however uncomfortable. The truly humble Christian is not an insecure doormat, but a person whose whole security is Jesus Christ. She does not pretend to have all the answers, but is always willing to learn. She puts love into action by not putting herself above others and by making what is good for the other person a higher priority than her own good.

If we want to reach the highest summit of humility then let us
set up that ladder on which Jacob in a dream saw angels
descending and ascending... . Now the ladder erected is our life on earth,
and if we humble our hearts the Lord will raise it to heaven.

Rule, Ch. 7

Let them make themselves strangers to worldly actions.

– Rule, Ch.4

SEPARATION FROM THE WORLD

This is the chief practice which distinguishes monasticism from other forms of Christian discipline. Separation from the world is not a pretended removal from the world: we are still people of our ambient culture, tied to it economically and in many other ways. Still less does it indicate a lack of care and concern for the world. On the contrary, we believe that by our prayer we touch far more lives than we could if we performed "good works" in the world.

The monastic enclosure enables us to create a very specific atmosphere. All the community, all our schedule and practices, are dedicated to the same goal: praise of, and union with, God. As our Constitutions say, our "Order is a monastic institute wholly ordered to contemplation." We choose to leave aside as many distractions as we can, to focus on this one goal.

By our silence we limit our contact with one another; by our enclosure we put even greater limits on our contact with family and friends, and above all on the surfeit of information and stimulation available through modern communication. We do not use television, radio, personal cell phones, social media. The advantages and temptations of the internet is something our whole Order is in the process of assessing, with many communities restricting internet access to certain hours of the day.

May the Father of Our Lord Jesus Christ enlighten the eyes of your hearts that you may see how great is the hope to which you are called.

– Eph 1,17-18

Our families may visit us once or twice a year, but we visit them only when there is a serious need such as a death in the immediate family, or when our parents grow too old to travel. And we are in touch by phone or mail only on a limited basis. But our community also has a very warm outreach to our families. When one sister's family is here, many of us will visit with them, so that we come to know and care for them personally. And as they experience the love and peace of our monastery, and see that we are normal human beings who enjoy a good laugh, our families come to love our community in return.

SOLITUDE AND COMMUNITY

All monastic life has a strong element of solitude because at the heart of prayer we are alone with mystery, "alone with the Alone." Yet as Christians we are part of the Body of Christ, and we believe that in prayer our unity with all people can reach its deepest level.

Cistercian/Benedictine monasticism is strongly communal: we live together, eat together, pray together, and often work together, day after day. The primary form solitude takes in our life is silence when we are together. But we also have space for physical solitude. Each sister has her own cell for sleeping, which she may also use for reading and prayer. In addition to our annual community retreat, we each make a private retreat in solitude; and we have a personal day of solitude each month.

Do you keep watch? He keeps watch also. If you rise at night before the time of vigil and hasten to anticipate the morning watch, you will find him there. He will always be waiting for you.

– *St. Bernard*

*Living in solitude and silence they aspire to that interior quiet
in which wisdom is born. They practice self-denial in order to follow Christ.*

– Constitutions of the O.C.S.O., 3.3

ASCETICAL PRACTICES

Among the most basic monastic practices are fasting, celibacy and vigils, ancient physical disciplines which are a great help on the spiritual journey. Fasting and celibacy aim at bringing order to our drives for food and for sexual intimacy, since when left undisciplined they can dominate our lives. But the heart of these practices goes well beyond spiritual athleticism. Like everything else in Christian life, they aim ultimately at making us better lovers: that is, they attack our selfishness at its most urgent level.

Fasting

Monastic discipline means being content with whatever is served, not eating between meals, and eating in moderation. Abstinence from meat is a central element of Trappist observance; but we are vegetarians by practice, not by moral conviction. In fact, when we come to the monastery we have to leave behind our personal preferences and practices, in favor of the common table. Our main meal is at noon, with a light breakfast in the early morning and an optional light supper in the evening. We keep the "winter fast" (Sept 14 through the end of Lent) by serving only soup and bread at our main meal on Fridays, and during Lent, on Wednesdays as well. Our food is delicious as well as nutritious, and our common dinner is a critical element of community life.

Celibacy

Christian celibacy complements the vocation to marriage and family; and like Christian marriage, it is a vocation, not merely a chosen lifestyle. Those called to be parents give the best part of their lives to the enormous task of raising children, who are this world's future. Those called to monastic life give their lives to a goal beyond the limits of this world, and are signs that the meaning of human life does not end here. We relinquish not only the joy of sexual intimacy, but also the joy of having children and family, because Jesus has inspired us with a deep desire to give our whole life's focus to seeking union with him.

Vigils

Prayer during the night was a practice beloved of the earliest Christian monastics. Early Christians kept prayerful watch all night before Easter, to commemorate the night on which Jesus rose from the dead, and to look for his final coming. Similarly, monastics keep watch for the Lord's return. And because it is the darkest and quietest time of the day, the time before dawn is particularly apt for prayer. But the practice of vigils is also about guarding one's heart at every moment, in order to let go of negative thoughts and feelings that distract us from loving attention to God and our neighbor.

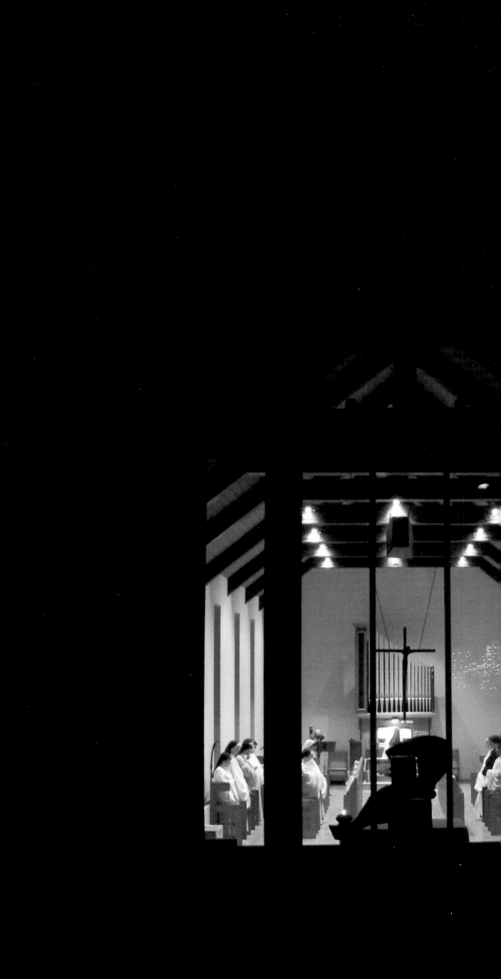

PRAYER

Prayer is at the heart of monastic life. Human nature is designed for union with God, and so in a sense, to pray is to do something very natural and human, something written into our make-up. To the extent that we love God, or simply want to love God, we want to pray, to be in relationship with God.

Most loving Jesus, may my soul choose to know nothing apart from you, that, disciplined by your grace and instructed by the anointing of your Spirit, I may progress well, passionately, and powerfully in the school of your love.

— St. Gertrude

Those of us who are followers of Jesus Christ want, specifically, to be in relationship with Jesus, to learn from him, to spend time in his company, to be intimate with the one who is nearer to us than our own hearts. This is what drives the monastic to spend such a large part of every day in prayer.

Much of our life is structured to minimize the obstacles to prayer of the heart. At first glance much monastic teaching on prayer seems to have little to do with prayer; certainly, little to do with method. The focus is first of all on growing in self-knowledge and in freedom from the various passions that dominate us and keep our eyes on ourselves, rather than where we want them to be – on Jesus.

And if we lack experience at prayer, monasticism has a wonderful cure: pray lots! Our whole life revolves around prayer: communal prayer, personal prayer, prayer in church, prayer outside church. Even after years of prayer, we may struggle with distractions; but we become, as it were, habituated to prayer. Our day is structured so that at least the problem of finding time for prayer is solved: it is built into the schedule, and is a communal, not merely personal, priority. Whether vibrant or dry, prayer becomes a necessity and a habit.

It is not possible to speak of Christian prayer without speaking of love. Ultimately, it is love for Jesus that keeps us going, and the measure of our prayer is not our achievement, but our desire. This love helps us take to heart the needs and sorrows of the world, the difficult situations in our own lives and in our families, and the many prayer requests we receive, to beg God's help but also to continue to praise and thank God whose love exceeds all suffering.

EUCHARIST

So great was Jesus' affection for his disciples, and so high his esteem for material reality, that he left us the gift of the Eucharist, the Christian ritual in which bread and wine become his body and blood, and we receive him in a way both physical and spiritual.

For early Christians Eucharist was a weekly event, but over the centuries in Western Christendom it became a daily rite, and so it remains for us: the central focus of the day, the communion with God, with each other, with all people, that goes beyond words. Normally our Mass is in the morning, but since the early 1990's we have had our Monday Mass in the evening. This is a better time for some of our local friends, so our Monday evening Mass is often the best attended of the week.

Our Constitutions say it perfectly: *"The Eucharist is the source and summit of the whole Christian life and of the sisters' communion in Christ. For this reason it is to be celebrated by the whole community every day. It is by sharing in the paschal mystery of the Lord that the sisters are united more closely with one another and with the whole Church."*

– Constitutions of the O.C.S.O., 18

Exposition

Every Sunday for half an hour before Vespers the Blessed Sacrament is "exposed" on the altar, and the community gathers for silent adoration. One Sunday a month is our Retreat Sunday, a day of extra quiet and prayer, with Exposition from after morning Mass until Vespers, with sisters taking turns being in church and praying.

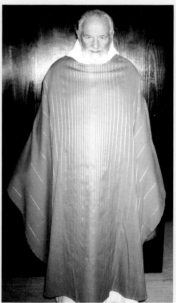

From 1964 - 2006 we had a chaplain, one of our brothers from New Melleray, living on our property. After 2000 their services were also supplemented by those of several diocesan priests. Our last three resident chaplains are pictured here.

LITURGY OF THE HOURS

Also known as the Divine Office, or the Work of God (*Opus Dei*), the Liturgy of the Hours brings us back to God and to prayer repeatedly during the day. All the Offices include a hymn, the chanting of psalms, and a reading from Scripture, and are meant to sanctify the different times of the day. Like the Mass, they also include antiphons (short chants that frame the psalms) and prayers. These change with the liturgical seasons – Advent, Christmas, Lent, Easter, Ordinary Time – and on feast days. One of the greatest joys of monastic life is that we are thoroughly saturated with these seasons, since our day is punctuated by well-loved antiphons whose beautiful tunes and texts tremendously deepen our awareness of salvation history. When it is Advent here, you really know all day that it's Advent!

The main anchors of the Office are morning prayer (Lauds) and evening prayer (Vespers), each about ½ hour long. In between are the three "Little Hours" (mid-morning, noon, and mid-afternoon prayer), lasting about 10 minutes.

The longest Office is Vigils, prayed during the final hours of the night. Our celebration of Vigils on a regular weekday lasts less than 40 minutes, but on Sundays and feasts sometimes an hour or more. Vigils begins only 15 minutes after we get up, so that our minds are engrossed in a long stretch of prayer just as they are awakening.

At the other end of the day is Compline, lasting about 15 minutes. While the elements of all the other Hours change with the seasons, Compline stands outside the liturgical calendar. Except for the addition of a few "Alleluia's" during Eastertide, it is identical night after night, and we sing it by heart. It reminds us that, beyond the linear progression of salvation history which all the rest of the liturgy celebrates, stands the unchanging eternity of God. You would think the extreme repetitiveness of Compline would make it boring, but somehow it is a favorite of many sisters and guests – and not only because we go to bed afterward! On weekends it is accompanied by harp, and every night concludes the day with the Salve Regina, an ancient chant in praise of Our Lady.

Terce (mid-morning prayer) at our candy factory.

Then comes the Great Silence, as we close our lips on speech and song until Vigils begins the new day with "O Lord, open my lips, and my mouth shall declare your praise."

PERSONAL PRAYER

Even outside the liturgy, we try to bring our minds continually back to God. Personal prayer may take many forms: centering prayer, dialogue with Jesus, the Rosary, quiet adoration and praise, pondering Scripture, interceding for people's needs. There are as many ways of praying as there are people, and even as individuals our prayer changes to reflect what is happening in our life – or in our day.

Each sister is expected to spend at least a half hour in private prayer during the early morning. And every day after Vespers we all remain in church for 15 minutes of silent prayer together, supporting one another in remaining faithful to our vocation to prayer.

See how hiddenly Christ prays, Christ who taught us to pray in secret to the Father. You too, make for yourself a hidden place within yourself, in which you can flee away from yourself and pray in secret to the Father.

– Isaac of Stella

We also spend time regularly in more familiar ways of reading. All are encouraged to read books of solid spiritual worth, whether classics or contemporary works. And we study, as well: the Rule of St Benedict, the vows, monastic history and spirituality, liturgy, Scripture, theology, etc. Newcomers have classes on these topics; senior sisters study to teach them, or to enrich their own spiritual lives. And we engage speakers to give lectures to the whole community.

In addition, at our noon meal the community is fed with words as well as food: one sister reads aloud from a book while the rest of us eat. These "refectory books," chosen by a rotating committee, cover a wide variety of spiritual and occasionally non-spiritual topics, with special books chosen for the liturgical seasons (particularly Advent and Lent).

Your word is a lamp for steps, and a light for my path.

– Ps 119 (118),105

MONASTIC WORK

What on earth do nuns do all day long when they are not praying? People sometimes imagine our life is very leisurely, with plenty of unused time. Actually, it is a constant struggle for us, just as it is for most people, not to be consumed by all the work to be done. The monastic discipline of laying aside the task at hand when the time for work is over does not come easily.

Some monastic traditions depend on alms for much of their day-to-day needs, but Cistercians place a high priority on manual work. St. Benedict calls the liturgy the *opus Dei*, the "Work of God," and he calls our labor the *opus manuum*, the "work of our hands." The tools of the monastery are to be treated with as much respect as the "sacred vessels of the altar" (Rule, Ch. 31).

Our work is always a response to community needs. We do not choose our own work. Instead, community jobs are distributed by the abbess. We also have a committee of sisters to look at community needs and fit them with sisters' capabilities. Our jobs are changed rather frequently, to help us maintain a detached attitude.

Some of our work is familiar to nearly everyone: cleaning, cooking, laundry, washing dishes. Like other home owners, we mow lawns, rake leaves, paint walls, wax floors, maintain appliances, take care of the landscape. We cut out and sew our habits, mend clothes, or answer the phone and the door. There is music practice for the organists and chief singers in our liturgy, and community choir practice, too. We have a large vegetable garden, a small herb garden, and fruit trees.

Some of us do pastoral work: teaching and guiding new members in the monastic way, caring for our sick or aging sisters, ministering to guests, giving spiritual direction, or assisting women exploring a monastic vocation. And there is administrative work: bookkeeping, correspondence, planning the liturgy, managing our farm and timberlands, overseeing the daily work, handling insurance, maintaining records and archives, etc. In addition to all this, nearly every member of our community helps with our candy industry, our primary source of income.

We may be asked to take on jobs quite different from the sort toward which we would normally gravitate; we may even be asked to do something for which we feel we have no skills at all. Here we need to rely on God's grace to see us through, and we grow in reliance on God more easily where we cannot rely on ourselves. Being stretched in new directions also calls forth unused parts of our personality and gives them space to flourish.

As we work, we participate in God's act of creation. Work that is unpressured but disciplined, that is done in the service of others rather than for one's personal aggrandizement or wealth, can be amazingly satisfying. We try to live simply, to make do with what is at hand when possible. Doing all this in an atmosphere of peace unleashes our natural creativity and adds another spark of joy to our work.

OUR CANDY BUSINESS

Each Cistercian monastery must find a way to support itself through some form of manual labor, and for most of our history agriculture has been the main work. For centuries Cistercians relied on a secondary work force: lay brothers and lay sisters, who did a large share of the manual work while "choir" monks or nuns spent longer hours in liturgical prayer. By the mid-20th century this division seemed both outdated and unjust, so the two types of Cistercian vocation were formally merged in 1965. An unforeseen consequence of this unification was that supporting ourselves by farming while maintaining a full schedule of prayer went from being difficult to being impossible.

In the past half-century nearly all our monasteries have switched to small industries, and with our agricultural background they are often food-related: candy, cheese, beer, chocolates... As the Western world moves from manufacturing to service industries, we have moved from agriculture to manufacturing! But for us "manufacturing" does not mean mass production. Instead, it enables us to continue to work with our hands, producing goods whose simplicity and integrity reflect the peace and order God can bring to human labor.

When Mississippi Abbey was founded in 1964, our founding house, Wrentham, still had a substantial farm, but also a flourishing candy-making business. Here in Iowa we tried our hands at a variety of small crafts: making wreaths, cookies, etc. But we needed something we could produce on a larger scale, and in 1965 one of our sisters returned to Wrentham to learn how to cook caramel. And we have been making our famous creamy caramels ever since!

Within a few years we started branching out with our own "product line." A local Dominican sister showed us how to temper chocolate and coat our caramels with it. This was in the days of grills and full habits, and Sr. Owen sat on one side of the grill in a tiny room with a little pot of chocolate, while two of our sisters on the other side copied what she was doing. Since that one lesson, we have been selling chocolate-coated caramels.

We have often experimented with other sweets: our "Irish Mint," a non-chocolate candy introduced in 1980; a chocolate mint, the "Swiss Mint," in 1987; and our hazelnut meltaway around 2002. These candies have a much simpler process than the caramels – they take a crew of only 1 person, where the caramels require teams of 5 or 6.

We sell annually about 60,000 lbs. of caramel products, and about 2,000 lbs. each of our other candies. Our business is extremely seasonal, with the vast majority of our sales made for Christmas gifts. As the caramels have a limited shelf-life, we have to produce the bulk of them in the months September to December, a time of year known to us as "Candy Season." Almost all our other work is put on hold while we go daily to make candy. Even this discipline has its benefits, requiring each sister to let go of other jobs for which she is responsible, in order to participate in the common work which earns our livelihood.

As our community grew, so did our business. Our original "candy house" was a large mobile home. In 1979 a friend in the construction business offered to double the size of the building, and added an attic for storage – all at no cost to us. This wonderful gift served us well for over 20 years, but eventually we needed a sturdier structure actually designed for manufacturing. For example, as large semi's replaced smaller delivery trucks, they could no longer get to our little loading docks; nor had we forklifts to handle pallets. When a delivery arrived, we would stop production, set some rollers in place, break open the pallets in the truck, and form a chain line to hand boxes up through a trap door into the attic! Thanks to the kindness of many donors, in 2001 we broke ground for a real factory, completed in the summer of 2002. It is beautiful and fully functional and enables us to support ourselves and our life of prayer. We thank God for this blessing daily.

Our candy business gives our community a common work, a time and place where we work together on a shared task. After the liturgy and the common table, common work is perhaps the most important element binding our community together. Candy-making is not always easy work; some of it requires heavy lifting, or else doing the same small actions over and over, which can be very wearing on the body, especially as we age. In this we feel our kinship with so many who labor with their hands.

Our business goal is not maximum growth, but simply to provide our living expenses. So we try to keep our sales level high enough to support us but not so high as to place great strains on the contemplative quality of our life – not always an easy balance to maintain. As our seniors have entered into old age, we have increasingly supplemented our work force with volunteers and employees. This trend is likely to continue, as we try to reduce the physical burdens on sisters who are aging or have other health problems.

Running our own business is hard work but also great fun. We try to work in a prayerful way and to offer products with a certain quality. And we can say in all honesty, we have never tasted any other caramels as good as our own!

First, the caramels are cooked in large copper kettles, around 90 lbs. per batch. As soon as each batch is cooked, it is poured and spread on a large marble or steel table where it cools overnight.

The caramel is very hot when poured, around 242°F.

The next day, the cooled caramel is cut into slabs and each slab is run through a machine which cuts it into strips.

The strips of caramel are put through a large and complex machine which cuts them into individual caramels – and (the tricky part) wraps them. The wrapped caramels are put into finished gift boxes.

Strips of caramel are run through a machine which cuts them into small squares.

Just before the newly coated caramels enter the cooling tunnel, a diagonal "squiggle" is put on each candy, by hand. We have been told this indicates that what's inside is caramel.

The caramel squares are fed onto a belt, pass under a flow of chocolate, then go into a cooling tunnel. Their journey through the cooling tunnel lasts 7 minutes.

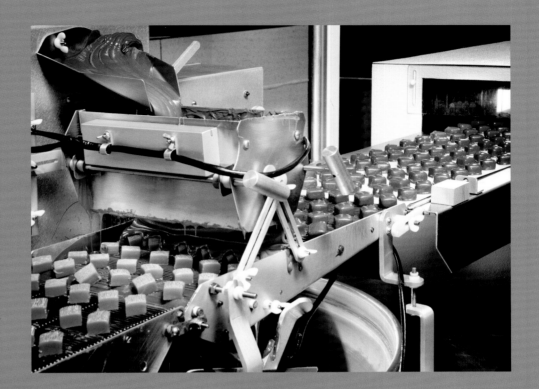

As the cooled candy comes out of the tunnel, it is put into gift boxes.

Pouring Irish mints.

Cleaning the corn syrup tank.

The completed gift boxes are shrink-wrapped and then packed into cartons, which are stacked on pallets.

Moving pallets.

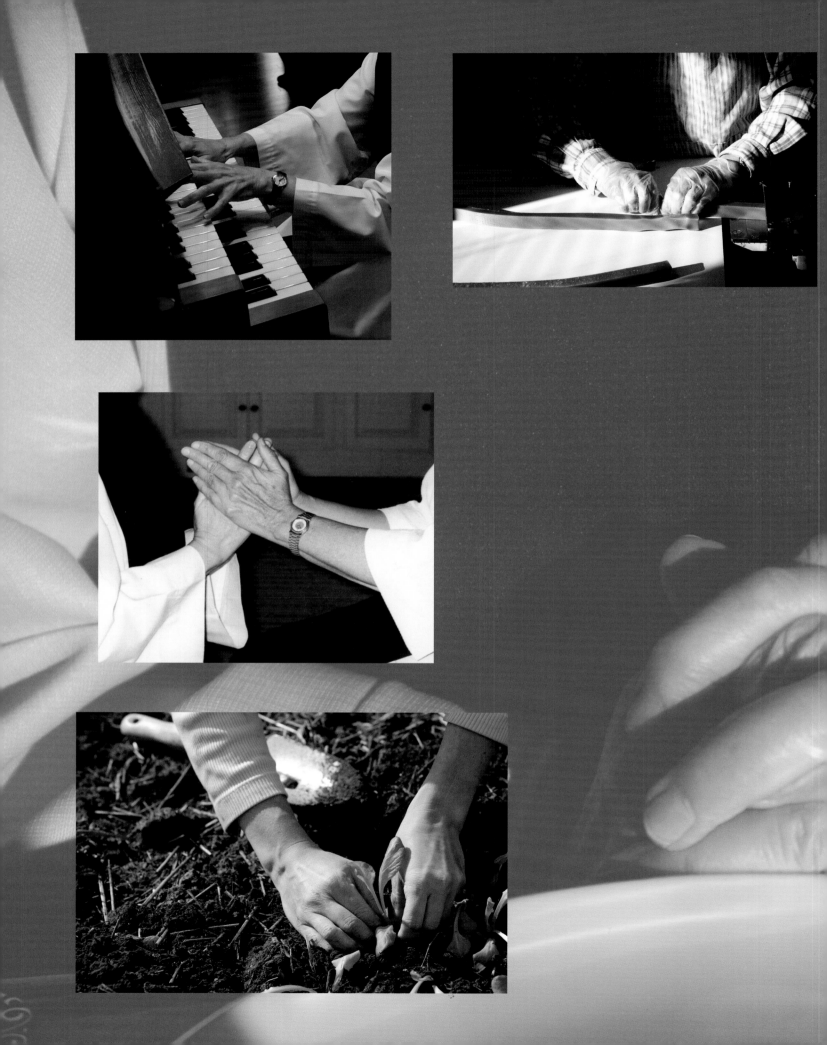

OUR LAND AND ITS HISTORY

Mississippi Abbey is located on the second highest bluff over the Mississippi River in the state of Iowa. The monastery buildings are on top, so we have a spectacular view for miles across the river into the hilly farm country of western Illinois and Wisconsin. Most of our 650 acres lie below these heights: over 350 acres of steeply rolling woodlands, a narrow creek valley with good pasturage, and about 200 acres in cultivation.

Artifacts found on our land: stone for grinding cornmeal, ca. 5 1/2" long.

Arrowheads, 2" long. Left: from a native group that inhabited Iowa about 2,000 years ago. Right: indeterminate age, possibly Middle-to-Late Archaic, ca. 3500-1500 BC.

The last group of Native Americans to live in our area were the Mesquakie (Fox), who settled in Iowa in the 18th and 19th centuries. Earlier native groups were already practicing some limited agriculture, so Iowa's farming history goes back centuries. Our land still has some Indian mounds; state archeologists have suggested that the Mound field was used as a summer camp for making stone tools, and from time to time arrowheads and grinding tools come to light. As recently as the late 1800's there was still a Native American who frequented our property. An old neighbor recalled that a relative of hers who lived in our Stone House would set out a pie or a loaf of bread for him from time to time.

The earliest European settlers were attracted to the upper Mississippi primarily by the presence of abundant lead ore. From the 18th through the early 20th century lead mining was a leading industry, and our land is still dotted with old mining holes.

European farm families eventually displaced the Mesquakie and cleared out large tracts of woodlands to grow crops. Settlers came to the Dubuque region especially from Ireland and Luxembourg. The Eiffes family of Luxembourg were the first Europeans to settle a part of what is now our land. They started with a log cabin, gradually added on rooms, and finally put on stone facing and stucco that reminded them of their homeland in Luxembourg – and also provided a very well-insulated home. This is now our Stone House, our oldest building, dating to the 1860's and a prime example of the Luxembourger "Stone Houses" in the area.

Some Eiffeses who grew up here. Left: Otto Eiffes, his bride, and their witnesses. Right: Mary Eiffes joined the Dubuque Franciscans and was given the name "Sr Hildegard." So we are not the first sisters of the property!

The Stone House. The Eiffeses chose the location wisely. To the right (south and west) a steep hill shelters the house. To the left (east) is a magnificent view (see chapter opening).

In 1853 Joseph and Angelina Manhart, natives of Switzerland, purchased the land that is now our "North Farm," the northern section of our property. They raised a family and constructed a farm home and buildings. One of the earliest buildings was a log cabin still on our property, possibly used briefly as a dwelling, then as other buildings were constructed, converted into a storage space. Built in the 1850's, it has superb craftsmanship. All the log corners were cut almost perfectly so that each log had a tight fit, with no gaps. The weight of the white oak logs resting on each other eliminated any need for nails.

After 30 years the couple sold the farm to their oldest son, Joseph A. Manhart, and his wife Agatha (opposite page, top), who in turn raised 10 children there (opposite, bottom). The Manhart family continued to live on their homestead and farm until 1950, when the property was sold to Thomas Stampfer. By the 1980's most of the buildings were gone and the log cabin was in poor repair. In 1989 we dismantled what was left, carefully marking the logs, and reassembled it next to our pond, giving it a new roof and porch.

Front cover of sales brochure for the Stampfer estate, showing the front of the house which became our monastery.

In the mid-20th century Thomas Stampfer, owner of the Stampfer department store in Dubuque, bought the Eiffes farm and began to buy neighboring farms as well, consolidating them into an estate he named Hickory Hill Farms. He built several excellent barns and a beautiful home which became the first monastery building in 1964, as Hickory Hill Farms was converted into Mississippi Abbey.

Our brothers of New Melleray managed our farm and woodlands during our early years, and in 1967 they sent Br. Placid Zilka to live on our property. After several years of restoring our cropland, farm buildings and machinery, he planted our first field crops, and soon we had a rotation of corn, soybeans, alfalfa and oats. Working from scratch, he designed our farm road on the

Br. Placid planted a large orchard on our property, including an apple tree on which he grafted 50 varieties.

highest levels of our fields so it would not erode. He established the contours for crop planting and set up grass waterways to minimize erosion in our sloping fields. Several sisters learned to drive the tractors and cultivate the soil, while the whole community helped to bring in the hay crops and to "walk" the beans (a final weeding by hand, when the beans grow too large for machinery).

In the mid 1980's Br. Placid returned to New Melleray. As we could not spare a sister full-time to replace him, we hired part-time farm workers to assist with planting and harvesting. For some years we continued moving in the direction of organic and sustainable use of our land, and in 1996 our farm was certified as organic. More recently, however, we have had to rely almost completely on renters, and are sad to say their crops are no longer organic.

During his nearly 20 years as our Farm Boss Br. Placid also planted a
substantial orchard and grape vines, and we continue to maintain and replace a
modest number of trees and vines. Our very first spring we started a large
vegetable garden, and ever since we have usually supplemented our diet with
our own green beans, tomatoes, asparagus, winter squash, zucchini, potatoes,
and other vegetables. By October our freezer is well stocked with tomato sauce
and apple sauce, and we have shelves of jams and jellies.

We have also raised various types of animals: sheep in the 1970's, angora
goats and then beef cattle in the 1990's, chickens in the 2000's; each time we
have had to discontinue them because our labor was needed elsewhere in the
monastery. But it is hard to live in the country and not raise some kind of
animals. Our latest venture is beekeeping.

Being so close to the river, our land is part of the Mississippi flyway, a major migration route for birds. In addition to transient birds more than 40 species nest each summer on our property – from common species like robins and house sparrows, to more exotic ones like bluebirds, buntings, kestrels and cuckoos. In the winter it's not unusual to spot an eagle circling near the monastery, looking for prey down below in the valley; and the hooting of great horned owls nearby sometimes accompanies us as we pray in the dark before dawn.

Both we and the guests who come here to be with God are immeasurably strengthened in our prayer by the peace and beauty of our land. We thank him for this great gift!

In the early 19th century, as steamboats and railroads reached Dubuque, the woodlands near the river were heavily logged to provide fuel for the ships and ties for the railroads. The Stampfers started reversing the trend by planting a Christmas tree farm, and during our first year here, our brothers planted thousands of Christmas trees and black walnuts. Over the decades we have made plantations of various nut trees, and of a variety of native species good for the wildlife. Several farm fields have now been reforested. Between 2005 and 2015 alone we planted over 50,000 trees.

For some years the sister in charge of our woodlands has had the assistance of a professional forester. Early in 2014 he selected 200 black walnut trees for harvesting. The big logs were left in stacks in our farm fields, and before they were collected we organized a little expedition to see this marvel. Naturally we picked a day when there was a blizzard blowing more snow on top of numerous previous falls. Our pick-up truck got stuck in a drift, we had to flounder through the snow to reach the nearest stacks, and visibility was so poor we could barely glimpse one or two of the other stacks. In short, we had a satisfying adventure!

In 1986 we planted native prairie grass and wildflowers along our entrance road. Our prairie grass field has flourished ever since. Every year or two we burn the dead grass in the spring, which helps the new grass to flourish.

For the creation itself will be set free from its bondage to decay and obtain the glorious freedom of the children of God.

– Rm 8,21

Give me, O Lord, the comfort of my wilderness:
a solitary heart and frequent communing with
you. As long as you are with me, O my God, I
shall not be alone.

– *William of St. Thierry*

HOSPITALITY

Hospitality has a long monastic pedigree. Benedictine and Trappist/Cistercian monasteries usually welcome guests into a special section of the monastery church, where they participate in the liturgy by listening and praying. There is usually a guesthouse too, where guests may stay for some days, sharing in the prayer and silence.

At Mississippi Abbey, all our liturgies are open to the public. We have never built a guest house but instead have taken advantage of small homes that were already on the property when we moved here, including the oldest building on our property, a lovely century-old Stone House with magnificent views of our land and far beyond. The Stampfers had a 2-family guest duplex which is now our Guest House and Retreat House. We provide food so those who are staying can prepare their own meals. This gives guests maximum privacy and flexibility in their schedule.

In 2003 we opened "St. Benedict's Welcome Center" in space made available by the construction of our new candy factory. The Welcome Center houses a small gift shop, a conference room where a sister may speak to visiting groups, and several small parlors where a sister can give spiritual direction.

Hospitality is always held in a careful balance with another crucial aspect of monastic life, which used to be called "flight from the world." Although this phrase is distasteful to most of us now, the reality it enshrines – constructing an alternative environment in which Gospel values predominate – finds a modern analogue in the more popular term "countercultural." Fidelity to our vocation to hiddenness, silence, and

All guests are to be welcomed as Christ, for he himself will say, I was a stranger and you welcomed me.

Rule, Ch. 53

prayer means that we put some boundaries between ourselves and our culture. The enclosure of the monastery is physical space normally reserved for the monastic community.

At the same time, many monasteries are searching for new ways to assist people as they struggle to find God in a noisy and increasingly secular world. Here at Mississippi Abbey we added two new forms of hospitality: a long-term guest program, and lay associates.

LONG-TERM GUESTS

In the early 1980's we began to allow women who desire a more intense experience of monastic life to join us inside the enclosure. It would be untrue to say this does not have some repercussions on our life. But it has been a small price to pay for the joy of sharing our riches with others who can profit from them. Nearly 100 women have participated in this program.

LAY ASSOCIATES

Formal association with lay groups is a new phenomenon in the Trappist world. In the mid-1980's the monastery of the Holy Spirit in Conyers, Georgia began the first such group in the United States. In 1994 they hosted a meeting to provide monks, nuns and their lay friends from other American Trappist houses with suggestions for starting similar groups. Since we and our brothers at nearby New Melleray were interested, as were some of our lay friends, we pooled our resources and formed one group associated with both communities. The first meeting of the Associates of the Iowa Cistercians was held in January 1995.

Our group began as an assembly of strangers, some of them with a history of alienation from the Church, many with limited experience in prayer. Yet something drew these people to the monasteries and touched the depths of their hearts. For 20 years our associates have committed one Saturday every month to a meeting at one of our monasteries. From the start the group has been open to the leading of the Holy Spirit, and it has been a joy to watch them form a genuine community and grow in habits of prayer and service, a blessing to acknowledge them as our very dear spiritual sisters and brothers.

THE WISDOM OF THE ABBESS

A major part of the pastoral responsibility of the abbess is to nourish the community with spiritual doctrine, and to challenge us to follow Jesus more closely. About once a week, with the community assembled in the chapter room, the abbess gives a short spiritual conference. In the following pages we include excerpts from these "chapter talks."

M. Columba (Margaret) Guare
1926 – 2009

Entered Wrentham 1951
Founding superior of
      Mississippi Abbey, 1964 – 1970
Abbess of Mississippi 1970 – 1982
Superior ad nutum of Stapehill Abbey,
      England, 1987-89

      Margaret Guare grew up in Montpelier, Vermont. After graduating from Trinity College in Burlington she began graduate studies in social services at Fordham (NY). A year later she left school to enter Wrentham, and was given the name "Columba" when she received the Cistercian habit.

      M. Columba guided us through all the struggles of establishing a new monastery and adapting to the post-conciliar renewal. After leaving office she went to Bolivia to help establish a House of Prayer among the poor, then served as temporary superior of our sisters in Stapehill.

      Sr. Columba's last 20 years were spent back in our monastery, where her ebullient creativity found outlets in designing vestments, singing in the schola, and writing poems for our Christmas cards. She continued to serve in all the simple activities of daily monastic life until she was incapacitated by her final illness (cancer). Her funeral was one of the best-attended events in our history, as family and many friends joined us in bidding her farewell – for now.

Feast of St. Benedict, March 1965

We are all familiar with the events in the life of St. Benedict: how as a young boy he fled from Rome which he found to be a city of sin and vice. He wanted God alone and so went to a cave at Subiaco for three years in a spirit of compunction. He had no visitors but the love of Christ triumphed in him and prepared him for his role of spiritual father. His first experience as Abbot was a failure. He returned to Subiaco and disciples began to gather around him. He moved to Monte Cassino and it was here that he fulfilled his role as Abbot and wrote his Rule. It was also here that he died in the arms of his monks.

St. Gregory the Great wrote the Life of St. Benedict and it was filled with stories of the miraculous. This was the style of that time. By this means he wanted to show the virtue of the man and how great was his union with God. But for us the reading of the Rule every day should teach us to know him. He did not do a lot of research as is the custom today – but at the end of his life from the fruit of his own experience Benedict wrote a guide for those who truly seek God alone. In it he tells us what he himself found necessary if one is to reach God: solitude, silence, poverty, prayer, penance – not extravagant corporal penances but mortification to bring the will into submission to the will of God. The chapter on humility is a record of his own progress in the virtue. The whole Rule is permeated with his supernatural attitude and spirit of faith. The monastery is to be a school of the Lord's service. All there must truly seek God. Nothing is to be preferred to the Work of God. God must be seen in the Abbot, the sick, the poor and guests. Everything belongs to God: tools as well as the sacred vessels of the altar. All must be done for the glory of God. Nothing is to be preferred to the love of Christ. St. Benedict is not just telling us to do these things but is revealing his whole interior life.

He has immense compassion for the weakness of human nature. Patient and kind, Benedict tried to make the life not too severe with adequate food and rest for the body. He wanted a light and joyous atmosphere – a family spirit. Nevertheless he was adamant in demanding the price to be paid to become a monk: complete self-renunciation, especially by obedience, humility and poverty.

We should be proud to have such a father, grateful too and we should turn to him for help in being monks. We can be sure he is interested in each one of us becoming a true monk, one who seeks God alone and prefers nothing to the love of Christ, and if we ask him he will obtain for us an understanding of his Rule and the grace to live by it.

M. Gail Fitzpatrick

1938 –

Entered Wrentham 1956
Founding member of
      Mississippi Abbey, 1964
Abbess 1982 – 2006

A native of Fairfield, Connecticut, Gail Fitzpatrick entered Wrentham shortly after graduating from high school. Sent to Iowa when we were founded, she served as our novice director from the time we began accepting candidates (1968) until she was elected abbess. Sr. Gail's pastoral gifts were quickly recognized throughout our Order, and she was one of the moderators at several of our General Chapters in Europe. (The General Chapter is a month-long meeting of the abbots and abbesses of the Order, held every third year, charged with the governance of our Order as a whole.)

Since leaving the abbatial office, Sr. Gail has held a variety of jobs in the community, including vocation director, junior director, and manager of our IT department. A selection of her chapter talks, *Seasons of Grace*, was published in 2000 by Acta Publications.

Julie Receives the Habit, Oct 14th 2001

Julie, this is a very important day for you and for all of us, the day when you receive the Cistercian habit and begin your novitiate in earnest.

When I was in the novitiate at Wrentham, Sister Andrew, my novice director, once told Mother Angela that she really wasn't too sure what she was supposed to be doing. M. Angela said to her: "Teach them how to be a religious as you would teach them how to play the piano." Sandra Schneiders in both of her books on religious life uses the same analogy: "Religious formation resembles the formation of a musician (or artist of any kind)." This seems especially appropriate for you, Julie, being the wonderful musician that you are.

Now, we might want to ask: what are you meant to learn? A person entering a Cistercian novitiate enters into a process of becoming a monk – of developing the gift of a monastic heart. A novitiate isn't a school where one gets a lot of information. One can study piano or voice as part of a well-rounded education. But if a person really wants to become a pianist as one's life call, that's very different. All of one's energy is concentrated on developing this skill, and it touches every aspect of the young musician's life – physical, mental, emotional, and even social. Most of all, to become a true musician requires practice, practice, and more practice. A sister of Clarke University told me that she witnessed a professional pianist, preparing for a concert there, practice one single run for two hours.

What does a novice in Cistercian Life practice? She practices the same things she will be doing for the rest of her life: prayer, lectio divina, community life, work, and humility. But most of all she learns how to love as a monastic woman. A monastic heart is a heart given totally to God. It isn't a question of felt ardor or passion. Sometimes God does allow us to experience love – God's love for us, for all creation – and our own deep desire to love in return. But it is the love that endures daily that is the important thing. Learn and practice the daily love. The monastic novitiate is a time when our heart can be freed to love as Jesus calls us to love - to love the Lord our God with all our heart, all our soul, and all our strength, and to love one's neighbor as oneself.

To practice love means to love others in Jesus' way. He just loves – he doesn't judge, he doesn't expect love in return, he just loves. I'm sure you know already, Julie, that love takes many forms in monastic community. It bears all things (even the sister who sings flat or sharp!); it forgives all things; and especially, love never loses hope. Love prays for others, for their happiness and well-being. Practice love now in the novitiate. Just as that famous pianist still practices daily, so too we can never stop practicing love. We can never think we've done enough, that we have it down pat. Love never ends; so, pursue love as the most important thing.

M. Nettie Gamble

1948 –

Entered Mississippi 1992
Abbess 2006 – 2012

       Born into a devout Presbyterian family, Nettie Gamble grew up mainly in Missouri and New Jersey. While completing an R.N. at Johns Hopkins University, she visited and then entered the Anglican convent of All Saints Sisters of the Poor in Catonsville, Maryland. After 20 years she left to enter the Catholic church, and two years later joined our community.

       By the time of her solemn profession in 1998 Sr. Nettie had already been chosen as one of the founders of our new monastery in Norway. She returned to Mississippi after two years at Tautra, and five years later was elected our third abbess. At the time of her election Sr. Nettie was our prioress and treasurer.

Second Sunday of Lent, March 2009

I find it interesting that Benedict put the chapter on the observance of Lent immediately after all the chapters that cover the daily life of a monk. Before RB 49, Benedict talked about prayer, reading, the Divine Office, abstinence, speaking and silence. All of this is to be important to us all year, but we cannot maintain this effort continuously. This inability is a part of nature. We cannot continuously breath in: we have to breathe out. Rain cannot always fall, nor the sun always shine, on one place. Life is a rhythm. We are not capable of the continuous force needed for continual movement, whether interior or exterior. Our life is one of alternations, with the sense of God's presence waxing and waning. It is in the little moments that we learn to be united with the Lord, becoming one with him, and the process is meant to bring us deep joy.

It is good to have this time of Lent to renew our desire, to make an effort to be present to God. There is nothing quite like denying ourselves in some little way that gets to us. If it is something little, we can more easily keep it in perspective. It is very good for us to experience the pain our ego feels when we let go of something so small. Isn't it humbling to see how much we can miss little things that we offer up for just 40 days, or how hard it can be to break a habit or form new ones even when we feel God's love asking it of us? And yet doesn't our soul feel greater freedom? We need this freedom to enter more fully into the Paschal Mystery of Jesus.

Lent is a time of healing, a healing not only of the ways in which we have given up or slowed down in our conversion of life, or the times we failed to love or surrender to God, but even more, a healing of the ways we do not trust in God's love and mercy. Paul says "He who did not spare his own Son but handed him over for us all, how will he not also give us everything else along with him?" Do we live as though we are going to receive, and indeed are receiving, the fullness of God's love and mercy? It is this fullness of God's love and mercy that is the fullness of life, a life in God, a life that is from God and exists in God.

This is the life that is reflected for us in the face of Jesus transfigured, a life that could not and would not be lost in suffering and death. It is our challenge to live in this paradox, that in the midst of and through our daily sufferings and deaths we live – indeed, it is Christ who lives in us and gives us fuller life. So in what ways is God working in us to conform us to Jesus? Our liturgy, lectio, prayer and daily life keep our eyes on Jesus, and the more we get to know him, the more we will recognize the work of the Spirit shaping us by the cruciform love of Jesus into the cruciform love of Jesus.

M. Rebecca Stramoski

1959 –

Entered Mississippi 1987
Abbess 2012 –

      Rebecca Stramoski grew up in San Antonio, Texas. After graduating from Southwestern Texas University with a degree in business, she studied for an M.B.A. at the University of Texas in San Antonio. She was the youngest of a large family, and her introduction to Trappist life came from visiting her brother in one of our monasteries. She entered our community when she was 26 and made her solemn profession in 1995. At the time of her election Sr. Rebecca was the novice director, grounds keeper, farm manager, and also maintained our candy machinery.

Second Sunday in Ordinary Time, January 2015

In the Prologue of our Rule, St. Benedict tells us that it is the Lord who seeks us and calls us to our monastic vocation. Benedict has all the action on Christ, which wakes us up to the fact that our call is a precious gift given to us. "The Lord calls out to us: Is there anyone here who longs for life…" and "what is more delightful than this voice of the Lord calling to us?"

We tend to think of our "call" as the big things like becoming a nun, getting married, or pursuing a career. But "the call" in today's readings tell us something different. Samuel's call from the Lord was simply…to listen! Andrew's call was to "come and see." Samuel's call was not "Samuel, be a judge for Israel" or "Your vocation is to be a prophet." Rather, through fidelity to this one action of listening, all these other things would unfold. If he had not been faithful to this call to listen, he never would have become a judge or prophet. These were secondary and contingent on that initial call. He did turn out to be the last judge for Israel and a prophet, but what made him great was his unwavering obedience and his loyalty to God.

Then we have Andrew's call to "come and see." He followed and found where Jesus dwelt, and from that moment on he spent the rest of his life "staying" with Jesus and "remaining" in Jesus. We learn through Andrew's example that if we want to know the mind of Christ, we need to stay close to His Heart.

Jesus had a call as well, and it too, was simply to listen – to listen to the Father. Jesus said "Everything I told you I heard from my Father" (Jn 15:15). His call was made up of dwelling and remaining in the Father: "I have kept my Father's commandments and remain in His love." He asks us to do the same.

All of us have the same call no matter what we are doing. If we are a nun or married or a waitress – our call is still to listen to Christ, to see and find Christ, and to remain in Him. But to answer this call we need three important qualities. We need to live as best we can, with much love, and with gratitude. So…

– Am I making a cheerful effort to live the common life in community?

– Do I show love through gentle actions and kind words? Am I approachable? Available?

– Am I grateful for my life as it is? It is good to remember that it is not joy that makes us grateful; it is gratitude that makes us joyful. What do I convey in my daily life?

Like Samuel, let us sit in prayer and listen to God calling out our name. What do you hear? And how will you respond? Like Andrew, let us see Jesus in our prayer asking us "what are you looking for?" What will be your response? Let us always try our best to be attentive to this invitation from the Lord, for as Benedict says, "What could be more delightful than the voice of the Lord calling to us!"

ARTS AT THE ABBEY

In the monastery, the arts, like all aspects of life, are at the service of God and the community. We have no great musicians, poets or painters who will leave a permanent mark on cultural history. But the life of contemplation increases our appreciation for beauty, and monastic life has always brought out the creative gifts of its members. There is no pressure to produce, no rivalry for honors, but an atmosphere where our humble talents may flourish and be of real use.

Being surrounded by nature, and singing God's praises several times a day, bring a strong element of beauty into our daily life. For special projects we enlist the aid of professional artists whose work will enhance the prayerful beauty and integrity of our monastery.

Medieval Cistercian churches are renowned for their awe-inspiring architecture – and for simplicity of style and absence of superfluous decoration. While the great stone edifices of the past would be far too costly to construct today, our churches are still characterized by architectural restraint, lack of color and ornamentation, and – we hope – a simple beauty.

Tautra Mariakloster

"Have patience that you may touch the beautiful. Become beautiful and then touch me; live by faith and you are beautiful. In your beauty you will touch my beauty with greater felicity. You will touch me with the hand of faith, the finger of desire, the embrace of love; you will touch me with the mind's eye."

– St. Bernard

Each year we send a community Christmas card to our families and a few friends. In the days before computers, we produced these cards by silk-screening. This card is from the 1970's.

My mother, my daughter, life-giving Eve,

Do not be ashamed, do not grieve.

The former things have passed away,

Our God has brought us to a New Day.

See, I am with Child,

Through whom all will be reconciled.

O Eve! My sister, my friend,

We will rejoice together

Forever

Life without end.

In 2003 one of our sisters drew this image of Eve and Mary for the feast of the Immaculate Conception, Dec.8. We all liked it so much that we decided to use it for our Christmas card the following year, and another sister wrote the poem to go in the card.

Fr. Richard John Neuhaus, editor of First Things, received a copy and wrote about it in the December 2005 issue: "I asked...an art historian...to check into it. While...the juxtaposing of Eve and Mary goes back at least to St. Jerome, an actual encounter between the two, never mind one in which Mary is consoling Eve, apparently does not appear...the Sisters of the Mississippi Valley [sic] have come up with something quite new [and] movingly suggestive."

A California composer, Frank La Rocca, read the poem in the magazine and contacted us for permission to set it to music. Frank visited us in 2008 for some local performances of his lovely setting, and a few years later returned to the Catholic Church. We started receiving requests for the picture and by 2012 were selling matted copies.

Philip Howie, the sculptor, and Our Lady of the Mississippi

In 2010 we commissioned Philip Howie, a sculptor from upstate New York, to make a bronze statue of Our Lady of the Mississippi. He completed the mold from which the statue would be cast shortly before Hurricane Irene struck; providentially, he was able to move the mold out of his workshop by wheelbarrow to save it from the floods. Unfortunately, a few days later Philip, still a young man, suffered a severe stroke. Some months later his wife Sasha was able to oversee the casting of the bronze statue, and to our delight both Philip and Sasha were able to attend the blessing of the statue on the feast of Our Lady's birth, September 8, 2012. The following year we built a garden and series of little waterways around the statue, using large pieces of limestone from our property.

The angels rejoice at a sinner's repentence.
And if my tears are a joy to the angels, what must my joy be?

– *St. Bernard*

Weekday Schedule

3:30	Rise
3:45	Vigils
4:30–7:15	Personal prayer, lectio
7:15*	Lauds and Mass
8:30–11:30	Work
9:45	Terce (prayed at work)
12:00	Sext
12:20	Dinner
1:00	Rest
2:00	None
2:15–3:45	Work
5:00	Vespers
5:30	Mental prayer
5:45	Supper (optional)
7:15**	Compline

Sundays and Major Feasts

3:30	Rise
3:45	Vigils
6:45	Lauds
7:15	Chapter talk
8:35	Terce and Mass
11:30	Sext
11:45	Dinner
12:30	Rest
2:00	None
4:30	Exposition
5:00	Vespers
5:30	Supper (optional)
7:00	Compline

*7 AM in the fall
** 7 PM in fall and winter

Beloved, we are God's children now; what we shall be has not yet been revealed. We know that when it is revealed, we shall be like him, for we shall see him as he is.

– 1 Jn 3,2

You shall be like him hereafter,
when you shall see him as he is;
then be like him now, too,
when you see him as he has
made himself for your sake.

– St. Bernard

151

Credits

A *Life of Hope*, published by Our Lady of the Mississippi Abbey, Dubuque, Iowa

Text: Kathleen O'Neill OCSO

Design and layout: Mike Meyer, and Sr Kathleen

Printing and binding: The Studley Press, Dalton, Massachusetts

Photographs: We are grateful to the many photographers who have generously given of their talents over the years. One of the joys of producing this book has been the opportunity to do justice to some of their work. The photographers' names and the page(s) on which their images appear are listed here (code: **T**op, **M**iddle, **B**ottom; **L**eft, **C**enter, **R**ight):

Don Blaeser   33T
Debbie Bowen: 91B, 93T, 94T, 94B, 95B, 149BL
Beth Campbell 24B
Sheryl Chen OCSO   38
John Cremons 50, 52-53, 57, 113B
Dana Downey 23T, 24T, 24B, 103B
Thomas Georgeon OCSO   137
Paul Green   10-11, 13, 75, 118-119
Richard Hayde 35
Ernst Herb   34

Sharon Kuttler 110-111
Benjamin Le SVD 122T, 122B, 124-125, 126-127
Bill Mannhardt 148TL
Alonzo McDonald 23B
Lydia Morvant 1
Miriam Pollard OCSO 140L
Brian Rooney OCSO   48
Bob Schwarz   8B
Ken Smith   95T
New Melleray Abbey archives 19 TL

David Peterson 8T, 9, 31, 58-59, 60, 69BL, 73, 82B, 87B, 88T, 96T, 98B, 99TL, 99TR, 99MR, 108, 138BR, 148MR, 149MR

Sisters of Mississippi Abbey: 6-7, 12, 42, 61, 62-63, 68, 71B, 76T, 76B, 77B, 83, 84, 92TL, 92TR, 96B, 109, 112T, 112B, 113T, 116T, 116M, 116B, 117T, 138TL, 148TC, 148ML, 150-151

Bill Witt. A special word of thanks to Bill Witt, who first visited us in 1997 to take pictures for an article in *The Iowan*, became a friend and then one of our lay Associates, and continues to photograph our monastery. Without Bill's beautiful work this book would not have been possible: 3, 4, 5, 14-15, 29, 36, 39 (all 6), 40, 41, 43T, 43B, 44-45, 46, 51, 54, 64-65, 67, 69T, 70TL, 70TR, 70B, 71TL, 71TR, 72, 74, 77T, 78, 80, 81, 82T, 86T, 86BL, 87T, 91TL, 91TR, 92B, 93B, 94M, 97T, 97B, 98-99, 98TL, 98TR, 99B, 100-101, 102L, 102R, 114-115, 117B, 120, 130, 136, 138-139, 138TR, 138BL, 141, 144, 145, 146-147, 148TR, 148BR, 149ML, 149BR

When not otherwise credited above, photos are from the monastery archives. Except for pp.19, 20T, 34, 38, 103T, 104, and 137 all photos were taken at Mississippi Abbey.

Text and photographs copyright © 2015 by Our Lady of the Mississippi Abbey

Photograph on p.107 courtesy of TH Media (*Dubuque Telegraph Herald*).

Our Lady of the Mississippi Abbey
8400 Abbey Hill Lane, Dubuque , Iowa 52003
www.mississippiabbey.org

Printed November 2015
ISBN 978-0-692-54816-5

I know the one in whom I have put
my trust, and I am sure that he is able
to guard what I have entrusted to him
until that Day.

– 2 Timothy 1,12

The question of hope lies at the root of what gives meaning to our lives. In the midst of the world's discouragements and distractions, the monastery is a beacon of peace and hope. Our Lady of the Mississippi Abbey is a monastery of Trappist/Cistercian women who have dedicated their lives to the praise of God in liturgy, silence and ordinary work.

Blessed with a beautiful location on a bluff above the Mississippi River in Iowa, the sisters share with us some of the joy and beauty of their home and their lives. In more than 170 color photographs, many by professional photographers, we glimpse something of the mystery of this way of life, so different from what we see daily in the media.

Christian monastics live out a tradition and practices developed over two millennia by men and women with a deep faith in Jesus Christ. The text includes a brief history of this tradition, a history of Mississippi Abbey, and sections on monastic spirituality.

monastery®

ISBN 978-0-692-54816-5

90000>

9 780692 548165